T0097884

MACBETH: A GUIDE

The Shakespeare Handbooks

MACBETH

A Guide

ALISTAIR McCALLUM

Ivan R. Dee

CHICAGO

Library of Congress Cataloging-in-Publication Data:
McCallum, Alistair, 1954–
    Macbeth : a guide / Alistair McCallum.
      p. cm. — (The Shakespeare handbooks)
    ISBN 1-56663-360-5 (acid-free paper) — ISBN 1-56663-361-3 (pbk. :
acid-free paper)
    1. Shakespeare, William, 1564–1616. Macbeth—Handbooks, manuals, etc.
2. Macbeth, King of Scotland, 11th cent.—In literature—Handbooks, manuals,
etc. I. Title.

PR2823 .M38 2001
822.3'3—dc21   00-066032

Introduction

In many ways, the plays of Shakespeare's time had a great deal in common with the movie scripts of today. Their prime purpose was to entertain. They were often written to tight deadlines and frequently involved collaboration between writers. Constant revision, cutting and rewriting were the norm. Considerations such as the available actors, current political events, and the changing tastes of the public always had to be borne in mind. Particular productions might excite interest and controversy, but plays were regarded as ephemeral and were rarely published in book form. The poet or essayist might produce a slim, finely bound volume in the hope of literary immortality, but the playwright worked and lived firmly in the present. Plays had not yet become literature. Theatregoing was a pleasure, not a duty.

Four hundred years later, a great deal has changed. Shakespeare is no longer simply a popular playwright; he has become a symbol, an icon. His name generates enthusiasm and anxiety in equal measure. Competing armies of literary critics - a profession unknown in Shakespeare's day - are engaged in a ceaseless war over his reputation and the meaning of his work.

I was lucky enough to grow up in Stratford-on-Avon and, as a regular visitor to the Royal Shakespeare Theatre, became familiar with many of the plays. Whatever else Shakespeare might be, he was not intimidating. The mist surrounding the plays gradually cleared; structure, characters, and ideas started to emerge; the creative input of actors, directors and crew became apparent. The better I understood the plays, the more absorbing and meaningful they became. Familiarity certainly did not breed contempt.

Without this degree of familiarity, approaching a Shakespeare play can be a daunting business. Where do we look for help? There is certainly no shortage of excellent books that discuss, interpret, and analyze Shakespeare's work. But for most of us the problems in approaching Shakespeare are essentially practical: the complexity of his plots, compounded by the obscurity (to modern ears) of his language. What was entirely missing, it seemed to me, was something to guide readers through these difficulties and give them the confidence to respond freely to the plays. This is what I have attempted to provide with the *Shakespeare Handbooks*. Each book gives a straightforward, detailed account of the plot, scene by scene, with plenty of quotations from the play itself, and help with the more obscure words and phrases. I have also included a handful of comments from writers of diverse periods, backgrounds, and opinions, which I hope readers will find thought-provoking, and a few pertinent facts and figures relating to Shakespeare's life and times.

Of course there is no single correct interpretation of a Shakespeare play. His plays were scripts, after all, for his own acting company, a close-knit group of men who worked together for many years; he wrote no introductions or footnotes, and precious few stage directions. The scenery and costumes, the movements and interactions of characters, the mood of the play—all these aspects, and many more, will always be matters for the imaginative judgment of those staging the play. And above all, the creative responses of spectators and readers will be many, varied, and unpredictable.

Shakespeare is challenging. His plays are rich, profound, and enigmatic. The experience of staging, performing, watching or reading them should be a journey of exploration. I hope that the *Shakespeare Handbooks* will give my readers help and encouragement with the first few steps of that rewarding journey.

MACBETH: A GUIDE

Setting the scene

Macbeth was probably written between 1603 and 1606. Shakespeare was about forty, and a leading member of England's most successful theatre company, the King's Men. The company's patron was King James I, who had just come to the throne, and who was both notoriously free-spending and a great lover of shows of all kinds.

A number of the new king's interests and beliefs - in the area of witchcraft, for example - are reflected in the play, and it was performed before the king on at least one occasion. In fact it is possible that the *Macbeth* known to us is an abridged version, specially prepared for the royal performance; the king is known to have liked his plays short. There has been much scholarly speculation about 'missing' scenes and events.

Regardless of the circumstances of its creation, the fact remains that *Macbeth* is a gripping, fast-moving, tightly-constructed drama, with a compelling, nightmarish quality that has consistently enthralled audiences through the ages. For a while, during the late 17th and early 18th centuries, songs, dances and special effects were included, and the language softened and refined: however, by the 1850s Shakespeare's dark, savage masterpiece had reasserted itself in its original form.

Macbeth has a unique reputation for bad luck, and many deaths, injuries, misfortunes and bizarre accidents have been associated with productions of the play. Superstition apart, it is certainly true that the play focuses our minds on the human capacity for evil, for choosing to act in ways which we know to be wrong; and this awareness is made so intense and terrifying in *Macbeth* that it can spread, at times, beyond the world of the play and the confines of the theatre:

"Macbeth, *which contains some of Shakespeare's greatest poetry, offers one of literature's most striking accounts of an individual soul's descent into the darkness of evil, and its resulting isolation from society. Macbeth's rejection of morality, and its consequences - the loss of his soul and the disruption of the society that he influences - horrifies us. This is a drama that is as terrifying as the plots and wars of real usurpers and kings."*

Charles Boyce, *Shakespeare A to Z*, 1990

Scotland in danger

The Kingdom of Scotland has been thrown into turmoil by a sudden, violent revolt. Its leader is the ambitious Macdonwald, whose aim is to defeat the army of Duncan, King of Scotland, and seize the crown by force.

Macdonwald is advancing steadily from his stronghold in the west. The conflict between the rebel forces and the King's troops is desperate and bloody. In the thick of the fighting are King Duncan's principal generals, the two noblemen Banquo and Macbeth.

Meanwhile, Sweno, King of Norway, is ready to take advantage of the disorder and invade Scotland from the east.

CURTAIN UP

A meeting is planned

I, i

As the battle rages, three witches meet on a stormy, deserted plain. In the midst of the thunder, rain and swirling fog, they make their plan: when the battle is over - which, they foresee, will be before the end of the day - they will come together once more, near the battlefield, to meet Macbeth.

Their intentions towards Macbeth are as yet obscure, but their enigmatic words do not bode well:

Witches Fair is foul, and foul is fair:
     Hover through the fog and filthy air.

News arrives from the battlefield

I, ii

At his military headquarters, King Duncan is waiting anxiously for news of the battle against Macdonwald and his rebel army. With Duncan are his two sons, Malcolm and Donalbain.

One of Duncan's captains comes into the camp. He has come straight from the battlefield, and is bleeding heavily from his wounds. Malcolm recognises him as the man who earlier saved him from capture by the enemy, and asks him about the latest state of the conflict.

The captain reports that, at one point, the two exhausted armies had reached a deadlock:

Captain   Doubtful it stood;
                    As two spent[1] swimmers, that do cling together
                    And choke their art.[2]

> [1] *fatigued*
> [2] *make it impossible for either to carry on*

If anything, luck seemed to be on the side of the rebels. However, Macbeth's intervention brought the battle to a swift, bloody conclusion:

Captain ... For brave Macbeth (well he deserves that
name),
Disdaining Fortune, with his brandish'd steel,
Which smok'd with bloody execution,
Like Valour's minion,[1] carv'd out his passage,
Till he fac'd the slave;[2]
Which ne'er shook hands, nor bade farewell to
him,
Till he unseam'd him from the nave to
th'chops,[3]
And fix'd his head upon our battlements.

[1] *favourite, protégé*
[2] *Macdonwald, leader of the rebels*
[3] *cut him open, from the navel to the jaws*

Their leader dead, the rebels broke up and retreated. However, no sooner had the battle been won than another threat to
the Kingdom suddenly arose: Sweno, King of Norway, sent an
invading force into Scotland, hoping to win an easy victory over
Duncan's battle-weary troops.

The captain reports that Banquo and Macbeth, when last
seen, were engaged in fierce fighting against this new onslaught.
The captain is by now fainting from his wounds: Duncan orders his attendants to help the man away to be treated by the
surgeon.

> *"The account given by the wounded Captain of Macbeth's con-
> quest of the rebels . . . is like a smear of blood across the first
> page of the play."*
> Harold C. Goddard, *The Meaning of Shakespeare*, 1951

"Macbeth *is compact, a perfectly rounded piece. It tells a strong story at great speed and takes the audience on a roller-coaster of excitement. You can see it a hundred times and it will still appear fresh. It is visually superb, which made me wonder what Shakespeare would have given us had Holly-wood existed in his time. The play is beautifully paced for the leading actor . . ."*

Laurence Olivier, *On Acting*, 1986

Scotland is saved

Ross and Angus, two noblemen, arrive at the camp with more news for Duncan. They confirm that a massive army has invaded from Norway. King Sweno himself has landed on Scottish soil: and it emerges that one of Duncan's own Thanes - noblemen granted land and power by the King - has assisted the Norwegian King in his bid to conquer Scotland.

Against all the odds, Macbeth, always in the thick of the fighting himself, has led the Scottish army to victory. Sweno has surrendered, and has been forced to pay a heavy ransom to retrieve the bodies of his slain soldiers for burial. The Thane of Cawdor, who had collaborated with Sweno, has been captured.

King Duncan is overjoyed that the threats to Scotland's security are over. He announces that the disloyal Thane of Cawdor must die; his title will be bestowed on the victorious Macbeth.

The witches demonstrate their power

I, iii

The three witches have gathered, as planned, to meet Macbeth.
A storm rages around them as they wait on a rough, wild heath.

One of the witches tells her sisters what has happened since
their last gathering. A sea-captain's wife has offended her, and
she is planning to make the captain suffer in return. His journey to the Mediterranean will become a nightmare of sleeplessness and hunger, and bad weather will keep him from his
destination for months:

1st Witch   I'll drain him dry as hay:
Sleep shall neither night nor day
Hang upon his penthouse lid;[1]
He shall live a man forbid.
Weary sev'n-nights nine times nine,
Shall he dwindle, peak,[2] and pine:
Though his bark[3] cannot be lost,
Yet it shall be tempest-tost.

[1] *eyelid*
[2] *become weak and emaciated*
[3] *ship*

Hearing the sound of a drum, the witches realise that Macbeth is approaching. They chant a brief spell, then fall silent.

A prediction

The fighting over, Macbeth and Banquo are making their way across the stormy heath in the direction of the King's palace in Forres. Macbeth notes grimly that the dreadful weather is not in keeping with the fortunate outcome of the battle:

Macbeth   So foul and fair a day I have not[1] seen.

>   [1]   *never before*

Suddenly Banquo notices the three sisters standing silently in the storm. He is startled by their wild, unearthly appearance, and questions them. They do not answer. However, when Macbeth asks them to speak, they greet him one after the other:

1st Witch   All hail, Macbeth! hail to thee, Thane of
                 Glamis!
2nd Witch   All hail, Macbeth! hail to thee, Thane of
                 Cawdor!
3rd Witch   All hail, Macbeth! that shalt be King hereafter.

Macbeth is stunned into silence. He is already Thane of Glamis, a title inherited from his father: he is ambitious for further power, but has kept his desires to himself. It is as if the witches have read his mind.

> "... the witches' function in the play is not so much to bring a whiff of brimstone across the stage as to symbolize the murky, unexplored reaches of the human mind ... Their first appeal is not to anything directly evil in Macbeth's nature but rather to the indecision, bewilderment and error which is their element and which they find echoed in his perplexity."
>
> John Wain, *The Living World of Shakespeare*, 1964

Banquo notices Macbeth's confusion. He addresses the witches again, asking them what they foresee for him:

Banquo	If you can look into the seeds of time,
	And say which grain will grow, and which will
	not,
	Speak then to me . . .
1st Witch	Lesser than Macbeth, and greater.
2nd Witch	Not so happy, yet much happier.
3rd Witch	Thou shalt get[1] kings, though thou be none:
	So all hail, Macbeth and Banquo!

[1] *father*

Macbeth now challenges the witches: there is no reason why he should be given the Thane of Cawdor's title, he says, and the idea that he might become King is beyond belief. He urges them to tell him how they have arrived at these strange ideas, and what they are doing on this stormy, deserted heath. But the witches refuse to say any more, and they vanish into thin air.

Macbeth contemplates his future

Macbeth and Banquo are left shaken and confused by the witches' strange words and sudden disappearance. They joke uneasily about what has just happened, and what the witches have promised them.

At this point two noblemen, Ross and Angus, arrive on the scene. They have been sent by King Duncan to break the good news to Macbeth; he has been made Thane of Cawdor.

Macbeth and Banquo are stunned. Within minutes, one of the witches' prophecies has come true:

Banquo	What! can the Devil speak true?
Macbeth	The Thane of Cawdor lives: why do you dress me
	In borrow'd robes?

Angus explains that Cawdor has been discovered to be a traitor; and that Duncan, hearing of Macbeth's bravery, has decided to reward him with the dishonoured Thane's title.

Out of hearing of Angus and Ross, the two generals talk again about the prophecy known only to the two of them. Banquo warns his friend to treat the witches' words with caution: he must not be influenced by the fact that one of their predictions has come true.

Banquo	. . . oftentimes, to win us to our harm,
	The instruments of Darkness tell us truths;
	Win us with honest trifles,[1] to betray's
	In deepest consequence.[2]

[1] *less important truths*
[2] *matters of greatest significance*

However, Macbeth cannot stop thinking about the prophecy. He was already Thane of Glamis: he is now Thane of Cawdor: if the sisters are right, he could soon be King.

To Macbeth's horror, he finds that the possibility of murdering King Duncan has already formed in his mind. The idea both appals and entices him, and he is so engrossed in thought that he cannot bring his attention back to his present surroundings:

Macbeth *[aside]* My thought, whose murther yet is but
     fantastical,[1]
    Shakes so my single state of man,
    That function is smother'd in surmise,[2]
    And nothing is, but what is not.[3]

  [1] *the thought of Duncan's murder, which only exists*
    in my imagination
  [2] *all my powers of action are crushed by the*
    overwhelming obsession in my mind
  [3] *the only things that now seem real to me are*
    imagined, potential or in the future

Macbeth tries to calm himself with the thought that he may
be destined to achieve his ambition without taking any violent
action:

Macbeth If Chance will have me King, why, Chance may
    crown me,
    Without my stir.

Finally managing to break away from his intense speculation, Macbeth apologises to his companions, who have noticed
that he is deep in thought.

Banquo and Macbeth agree that they must talk further, when
the time is right, about the strange scene they have witnessed.
Accompanied by Angus and Ross, the two generals now make
their way to the King's palace.

Duncan announces his successor

I, iv

The Thane of Cawdor has been executed for supporting the King of Norway in his failed invasion. Duncan's son Malcolm has received news of the execution from an eyewitness. The condemned man is reported to have behaved calmly and honourably:

Malcolm   . . . very frankly he confess'd his treasons,
Implor'd your Highness' pardon, and set forth
A deep repentance. Nothing in his life
Became him like the leaving it . . .

Duncan remarks that it is difficult to judge someone's true character by appearances. He thought he had known the treacherous Cawdor well:

Duncan   There's no art
To find the mind's construction[1] in the face:
He was a gentleman on whom I built
An absolute trust . . .

> [1] *there is no sure way of establishing a person's true feelings*

At this moment Macbeth enters, along with Banquo and the two noblemen. Duncan is overcome with gratitude and admiration for the two generals who have saved Scotland from destruction. Macbeth insists that they were simply doing their duty, and deserve no special praise; but Duncan says that he intends to single them out for special honours and rewards.

Tearful with joy and relief, and determined to share the happiness of the victory, King Duncan now makes an announcement: his eldest son Malcolm is to inherit his estate and title. When Duncan dies, Malcolm will become King.

Macbeth is Duncan's cousin; but any hopes of obtaining the throne lawfully are immediately dashed. He realises that he can only become King through violent action. He desperately wants the witches' prediction to come true, but the acts that will make it possible must happen in total darkness and secrecy:

Macbeth   [aside] Stars, hide your fires!
Let not light see my black and deep desires;
The eye wink at the hand;[1] yet let that be,
Which the eye fears, when it is done, to see.

[1] *Let the eye be blind to the actions of the hand*

King Duncan proposes a visit to Macbeth's castle in Inverness. Macbeth sets off ahead to tell his wife of the news, and to prepare for the King's visit.

> *"Duncan's generous and trusting nature contrasts strikingly with the evil which surrounds Macbeth . . . he is an important symbol of the values that are to be defeated and restored in the course of the play . . . Duncan's faith, misplaced first in the rebellious Cawdor and then in Macbeth, provides the audience with an introduction to the atmosphere of betrayal that exists throughout the world of the play."*
>
> Charles Boyce, *Shakespeare A to Z*, 1990

"Repentance is always close at hand, but Macbeth rejects it . . . Macbeth is trying to kill his soul, which as resolutely refuses to die. Guilt joins forces with grace to prompt him to repent but he will not."

Germaine Greer, *Shakespeare*, 1986

Lady Macbeth sees what must be done

I, v

At the castle in Inverness, Lady Macbeth is reading a letter from her husband. It describes, in excited terms, the three witches and their prophecy that Macbeth will be King.

Lady Macbeth guesses, correctly, that her husband has been hesitating over the action that needs to be taken. She herself has no doubts whatsoever: if the chance to take the throne presents itself, they must seize it. They must not let sympathy or sentimentality prevent them from achieving their ambition, even if it means that lives must be sacrificed.

She realises that her husband will need firm, determined guidance from her if he is to achieve the goal that they both desire:

Lady Macbeth   Yet do I fear thy nature:
                  It is too full o'th'milk of human kindness,
                  To catch the nearest way.[1] Thou wouldst be
                        great;
                  Art not without ambition, but without
                  The illness should attend it . . .[2]

[1] *to take the most direct route*
[2] *the wickedness that should complement your ambition*

A messenger rushes in to tell Lady Macbeth that King Duncan will be at Inverness castle this very evening. Lady Macbeth is exultant. This is their opportunity: they must not miss it. She prays that her determination to carry out the murder will not weaken. Like her husband, she wants the necessary deed to be done in complete darkness and secrecy:

Lady Macbeth   Come, you Spirits
                That tend on mortal thoughts, unsex me[1] here,
                And fill me, from the crown to the toe, top-full
                Of direst cruelty . . .
                                          Come, thick Night,
                And pall thee[2] in the dunnest[3] smoke of Hell,
                That my keen knife see not the wound it
                     makes,
                Nor Heaven peep through the blanket of the
                     dark,
                To cry, 'Hold, hold!'

    [1]   *remove any womanly feelings*
    [2]   *wrap, enshroud yourself*
    [3]   *darkest, gloomiest*

Macbeth now returns. His earlier excitement has subsided,
and he is quiet and apprehensive. His wife urges him not to let
his anxiety show: they must be relaxed, friendly and welcom-
ing when their guest arrives.

Neither of them talks directly of murdering the King, but
Lady Macbeth makes it clear that it must be done, and that she
will make the necessary preparations:

Lady Macbeth   . . . bear welcome in your eye,
                Your hand, your tongue: look like th'innocent
                     flower,
                But be the serpent under't. He that's coming
                Must be provided for; and you shall put
                This night's great business into my
                     dispatch . . .[1]

    [1]   *control; execution*

Macbeth is still uneasy. His wife again urges him not to betray any signs of emotion in his face. As long as they both remain calm and resolute, they will reach their goal: supreme power, over the entire nation, for the rest of their lives.

> *"He who seeks happiness for himself by making others unhappy is bound in the chains of hate, and from these he can never be free."*
>
> *The Dhammapada*, Buddhist teachings, 3rd Century B.C.

Lady Macbeth welcomes the King

I, vi

King Duncan arrives at Macbeth's castle. With him are Banquo, his sons Malcolm and Donalbain, and his Thanes and noblemen.

It is a calm, pleasant summer's evening. Countless birds, which have built their nests in every nook and cranny of the castle walls, are swooping through the warm air. As they approach, Duncan and Banquo are enchanted by the tranquillity and luxuriance of the scene:

Duncan	This castle hath a pleasant seat;[1] the air
	Nimbly and sweetly recommends itself
	Unto our gentle senses.
Banquo	This guest of summer,
	The temple-haunting martlet,[2] does approve,
	By his loved mansionry,[3] that the heaven's breath
	Smells wooingly here: no jutty, frieze,
	Buttress, nor coign of vantage, but this bird
	Hath made his pendent bed, and procreant cradle . . .

[1] *setting, situation*
[2] *house-martin, often nesting in churches*
[3] *by lovingly building his home here*

Lady Macbeth comes out to greet her guests. She is gracious and deferential as she thanks the King for his presence at the castle.

Duncan enquires after Macbeth, who has not come out with his wife, but she evades the question. She leads the King indoors, assuring him that everyone and everything in their castle is at his disposal.

> *"Watching* Macbeth, *every member of the audience knows that the possibility of becoming a Macbeth exists in his nature."*
>
> W. H. Auden, *The Dyer's Hand*, 1963

Macbeth considers the consequences

I, vii

A banquet is taking place in honour of the King. Macbeth, racked with doubts and fears about the planned murder, has left early.

He is now alone, trying desperately to clarify his thoughts about the situation he is in. He wishes he could be certain that the murder would be simple and final, with no unwanted consequences, reprisals, or complications. If this were so, the deed could be done swiftly, and the horror of the killing forgotten forever. The risk of punishment in the afterlife would be well worth taking:

Macbeth	If it were done, when 'tis done, then 'twere well
	It were done quickly: if th'assassination
	Could trammel up the consequence . . .[1]
	. . . that but this blow
	Might be the be-all and the end-all - here,
	But here, upon this bank and shoal of time,[2]
	We'd jump the life to come.[3]

[1] *trap its own consequences in a net, so they could not escape*
[2] *in this human existence, which is no more than a shallow sandbank in the sea of time*
[3] *ignore the risk of suffering in the next world*

But Macbeth knows that this is wishful thinking. The murder is bound to have repercussions. Besides, he reflects, the act is wrong in itself: Duncan is his ruler, his cousin and his guest. As King, he has been humble, mild and innocent of any wrongdoing.

Macbeth fears that natural justice will not allow the act to go unpunished. He visualises the forces of goodness rising up in accusation against him, however secretly the murder is committed, and spreading the news to a horrified population:

Macbeth   . . . his virtues
     Will plead like angels, trumpet-tongu'd, against
     The deep damnation of his taking-off;[1]
     And Pity, like a naked new-born babe,
     Striding the blast, or heaven's Cherubins, hors'd
     Upon the sightless couriers[2] of the air,
     Shall blow the horrid deed in every eye,
     That tears shall drown the wind.

[1] *killing*
[2] *invisible messengers, winds*

"Macbeth's soliloquies are raw, sensory, visual and profoundly irrational. They constitute Shakespeare's supreme achievement in self-expression . . ."

Levi Fox, *The Shakespeare Handbook*, 1987

Macbeth is persuaded

Macbeth's wife comes in, angrily demanding to know why he has left the banquet; the King has noticed his absence. Macbeth tells her flatly that he has changed his mind: the assassination must not go ahead. He is satisfied with the honours, gratitude and esteem which he has gained in the recent wars, and wishes to enjoy them rather than risk everything to become King.

Lady Macbeth accuses her husband of cowardice, reminding

him of his earlier excitement at the prospect of power. His man-hood, and his love for her, are clearly worthless if he gives up so easily. The opportunity has presented itself, and the time is right. If he does not act now to achieve his ambition, she will never again have any respect for him.

In the same situation, she says, she would have no second thoughts. However terrible the act, she would stand by her promise:

Lady Macbeth   I have given suck, and know
How tender 'tis to love the babe that milks me:
I would, while it was smiling in my face,
Have pluck'd my nipple from his boneless
    gums,
And dash'd the brains out, had I so sworn
As you have done to this.

Macbeth's earlier resolve to abandon the murder is already weakening. No longer concerned with the morality of the act, he repeats to Lady Macbeth his greatest fear; that things may go wrong, with dreadful consequences. She laughs off the idea. All they need is courage and determination.

Lady Macbeth now outlines her plan. The murder must be committed tonight: the King plans to leave tomorrow, so there will not be a second chance. She intends to get his two manser-vants drunk, to the point where they are both in a stupor. Dun-can will be sleeping soundly after his long journey, and she and her husband will be free to act:

Lady Macbeth   . . . when in swinish sleep
Their drenched natures lie, as in a death,
What cannot you and I perform upon
Th'unguarded Duncan?

The blame can be put upon the drunken servants. Macbeth is immediately taken with the idea. Blood from the dead King can be smeared over the two men as evidence of their guilt:

Macbeth   Will it not be receiv'd,[1]
                        When we have mark'd with blood those sleepy
                              two
                        Of his own chamber, and us'd their very
                              daggers,
                        That they have done't?
Lady Macbeth   Who dares receive it other . . .

[1] *accepted, believed*

Throughout all their exchanges, the two of them have avoided stating the truth directly; that Duncan is to be stabbed to death, in his bed, tonight, by Macbeth. Nevertheless, the plan is now in place, and there is no turning back. They return to the banquet together, determined to present an appearance of genial hospitality.

> *"Ironically, it is cowardice that finally drives him to resolve upon committing the murder: he is too cowardly to endure the name of coward from his wife."*
>
> Alan Hobson, *Full Circle: Shakespeare and Moral Development*, 1972

An unexpected meeting

II, i

It is after midnight, and within Macbeth's castle it is pitch-dark. Banquo and his son Fleance are preparing to retire for the night, and are making their way to their rooms.

Banquo is still troubled by the witches' prophecy. Despite his weariness, he is not ready for sleep: he knows that the sisters' prediction - that he will be the father of Kings - will continue to tempt and confuse him.

A sudden sound startles Banquo. Someone else is moving around quietly nearby, and Banquo grabs his sword from Fleance. The torchlight reveals that it is Macbeth. Banquo is surprised that his friend has not yet gone to bed, and mentions that King Duncan is already asleep. The King has been in excellent spirits all day, says Banquo: he has given generous presents to Macbeth's household staff, and a diamond to Lady Macbeth. Banquo then raises the subject which is uppermost in his mind. Initially Macbeth refuses to be drawn:

Banquo	I dreamt last night of the three Weïrd Sisters:[1]
	To you they have show'd some truth.
Macbeth	I think not of them . . .

[1] *sisters who govern human destiny: the three witches*

Macbeth then suggests, casually, that they should talk over the matter when they both have an hour or so to spare. He hints that, if the witches' prophecy is true, Banquo would do well to support him when the time comes for a new King to be chosen. Banquo replies, guardedly, that he is always willing to listen to advice as long as his honour and loyalty are not compromised.

The two men bid one another goodnight, and Banquo and his son retire for the night.

The time to act approaches

Macbeth and his wife have agreed on a signal to show when the time for the murder has come. Once Duncan's attendants are in a drunken stupor, Lady Macbeth will ring a bell. To avert suspicion, Macbeth now instructs his servant to remind Lady Macbeth that he is expecting the bell to ring when his drink is ready. The servant leaves to pass the message on to his mistress.

Macbeth is now alone, waiting for the bell. His fevered imagination starts to conjure up vivid, disturbing images:

Macbeth   Is this a dagger, which I see before me,
           The handle toward my hand? Come, let me
              clutch thee: -
           I have thee not, and yet I see thee still.

He becomes terrifyingly aware of the darkness enveloping the world, and the sleep, death, deception and witchcraft that the darkness brings. He walks apprehensively in the direction of Duncan's room:

Macbeth   Thou sure and firm-set earth,
           Hear not my steps, which way they walk, for
              fear
           Thy very stones prate of[1] my where-about . . .

    [1] *talk about, reveal*

Finally he pulls himself together, realising that the constant flow of images and words running through his mind only serves to make the action more difficult. The bell rings.

Macbeth   I go, and it is done: the bell invites me.
Hear it not, Duncan; for it is a knell
That summons thee to Heaven, or to Hell.

"Darkness, we may even say blackness, broods over this tragedy . . . the atmosphere of Macbeth, *however, is not that of unrelieved blackness. On the contrary,* Macbeth *leaves a decided impression of colour; it is really the impression of a black night broken by flashes of light and colour, sometimes vivid and even glaring . . . And, above all, the colour is the colour of blood."*

A. C. Bradley, *Shakespearean Tragedy*, 1904

A traumatic event

II, ii

Lady Macbeth, having rung the bell, waits for her husband's return. She has been drinking with Duncan's two manservants, and the drink has made her confident and exhilarated despite her nervousness. To ensure that the servants are unconscious, she reveals, she has drugged their drinks.

A sudden cry makes her jump: but it was just the shriek of an owl. She reassures herself that everything is properly prepared, but is shaken again when she hears Macbeth call out. She fears that something has gone wrong despite her careful preparations, and reflects, in a moment of vulnerability, that she could not have carried the plan to completion herself:

Lady Macbeth I laid their daggers[1] ready;
He could not miss 'em. - Had he not resembled
My father as he slept, I had done't.

[1] *the daggers of Duncan's servants, for Macbeth*

Macbeth returns, grim and agitated. He has carried out the murder, but is terrified that someone may have heard something suspicious. As he entered the chamber, he says, Duncan's sons in the next room woke up and, half-conscious, prayed aloud before falling asleep again. Macbeth is tormented by the fact that he could not join them in their prayers.

His wife tries to dissuade him from going over the events in his mind, but he cannot stop. His imagination becomes more and more frenzied and fearful:

Macbeth   Methought, I heard a voice cry, 'Sleep no more!
           Macbeth does murther Sleep,' - the innocent
               Sleep;
           Sleep, that knits up the ravell'd sleave[1] of care,
           The death of each day's life, sore labour's bath,
           Balm of hurt minds . . .

> [1]   *straightens out the tangled threads*

Lady Macbeth notices that he still has the two bloodstained daggers with him. She reminds him that they should have been left next to the sleeping servants, and tells him to go back and put the daggers in place.

Making no attempt to hide his fear, Macbeth flatly refuses to return to the scene of the murder. His wife grabs the daggers impatiently. The sleeping men must not only be in possession of the daggers, she reminds him, but smeared with Duncan's blood. She hurries off to complete the task herself.

Just after she has left, the silence of the night is broken by a loud, insistent knocking at the castle gate. Macbeth jumps with fright. He is dismayed at his fearful reaction, and realises that he is losing his self-control. He looks despondently at his bloody hands:

Macbeth   Will all great Neptune's ocean wash this blood
           Clean from my hand? No, this my hand will
               rather
           The multitudinous seas incarnadine,[1]
           Making the green one[2] red.

> [1]   *turn all the world's oceans the colour of blood*
> [2]   *totally, uniformly*

Lady Macbeth returns. Her hands too are now covered in blood. She sees that her husband is transfixed with fear and guilt, and urges him to come back with her to their chamber: they can wash off the blood and put on their nightgowns, and there will be no trace of evidence against them. There is no time to lose; the knocking at the gate is continuing, and there will soon be activity in the castle.

It dawns on Macbeth that he will only be able to come to terms with what he has done by cutting himself off from his persistent feelings of doubt and regret. The killing of Duncan has changed everything. He observes, grimly, that murder cannot be undone:

Macbeth   To know my deed, 'twere best not know myself.
            [*Knock.*]
            Wake Duncan with thy knocking: I would thou
               couldst!

> "*Throughout his rationalized insanity, neither Macbeth nor the audience ever gets a glimpse of what is driving him to what he is doing. The possessing demon never reveals its hand.*"
>
> Ted Hughes, *Shakespeare and the Goddess of Complete Being*, 1992

The porter takes his time

II, iii

The knocking at the gate continues. The porter, who was up drinking into the small hours, is slow to arrive. When he does, he playfully imagines himself to be the porter at the gates of Hell. He envisages some of the new arrivals he would be asked to let in; there would be no end of turning the key.

First comes a farmer, whose sin was to commit suicide when he realised that a plentiful harvest was due; his store of grain, carefully hoarded to make his fortune, was suddenly worthless.

Next comes a religious activist who, on trial for treason, swore his innocence: confronted with absolute proof of his guilt, he changed his plea, whilst maintaining that his earlier plea was morally justified at the time. He was hanged all the same, and could not argue his way into heaven.

Finally comes an English tailor who tried to make a quick profit by passing off trimmed-down French hose as the genuine article.

The porter eventually tires of his little pageant of imaginary sinners, and opens the gate. Macduff and Lenox, two noblemen of Duncan's court, are outside. They have been knocking at the gate for a long time, and ask the porter why he was not up earlier. Letting them in, he explains that he was drinking all night with his companions. To the visitors' amusement, he describes the effects of alcohol in some detail:

Porter	. . . drink, Sir, is a great provoker of three things.
Macduff	What three things does drink especially provoke?
Porter	Marry, Sir, nose-painting, sleep, and urine. Lechery, Sir, it provokes, and unprovokes: it provokes the desire, but it takes away the performance . . . and, giving him the lie,[1] leaves him.
Macduff	I believe, drink gave thee the lie last night.

[1] *knocking a man down, laying him out*

Macduff asks the porter if his master, Macbeth, is up. Before he can answer, Macbeth himself comes down to greet the new arrivals.

"*Macduff, knocking at the door on his errand to arouse the King, is in fact sounding the first note of retribution for a crime of which he is unaware, and which it will be his mission to avenge.*"

Robert Speaight, *Shakespeare: The Man and his Achievement*, 1977

The Gunpowder Plot - the unsuccessful attempt to blow up King James I and Parliament, prevented at the last minute on November 5th, 1605 - was at the forefront of the public mind at the time of *Macbeth*. The religious activist on his way to Hell is almost certainly a topical reference to Father Garnet, an English Jesuit priest hanged in 1606 for complicity in the plot.

At Father Garnet's trial, there had been lengthy argument about the permissibility of 'equivocation', the use of ambiguous, misleading language in order to avoid outright lying. Most observers were outraged at the defendant's attempts to escape the charge of perjury by claiming the right to equivocate:

"Equivocation excited an indignation much greater than a self-defending lie would have done, even adding to the language the abusive adjective 'Jesuitical' to describe duplicitous behaviour. Today's alternative, a marrying of diplomacy with the politics of power, is to be 'economical with the truth' . . ."

Peter Thomson, *Shakespeare's Professional Career*, 1992

The murder comes to light

Macduff asks if the King is awake yet, and explains that he has come to the castle early at Duncan's own request. Macbeth, outwardly calm and cheerful, shows Macduff to Duncan's quarters. He then comes back down to talk to Lenox, who comments on the dreadful night that has just passed:

Lenox	The night has been unruly: where we lay,
	Our chimneys were blown down; and, as they say,
	Lamentings heard i'th'air; strange screams of death . . .
	. . . some say, the earth
	Was feverous, and did shake.
Macbeth	'Twas a rough night.

Macduff rushes down from Duncan's chamber, screaming in horror. Barely able to describe what he has discovered, he urges Macbeth and Lenox to see the appalling sight for themselves. They run up to the King's room, and Macduff cries out frantically for everyone to wake from their sleep.

Lady Macbeth comes out, but Macduff at first refuses to tell her what has happened, fearing that she would find the shock unbearable. Banquo arrives next, and is devastated when Macduff breaks the news to him.

Macbeth and Lenox now return from Duncan's chamber. Unlike the reactions of the others, Macbeth's lament for the dead King is calm and measured:

Macbeth	Had I but died an hour before this chance,[1] I had liv'd a blessed time; for, from this instant, There's nothing serious in mortality; All is but toys . . .[2]

[1] *misfortune*
[2] *trifles, trivialities*

Duncan's sons, Malcolm and Donalbain, are the next to awake. Lenox tells them that Duncan's two manservants appear to have committed the murder. Apart from the bloodstained knives next to them, and the blood on their hands and faces, they were behaving strangely: they were only half-conscious, and were confused and incoherent.

Macbeth now reveals that he has just killed the two servants. Macduff turns on him furiously: without them, the truth about the murder cannot be established. Macbeth claims that his passionate loyalty to Duncan overcame his reason, and he could not stop himself. His words are contrived and unconvincing:

Macbeth	Here lay Duncan, His silver skin lac'd with his golden blood; And his gash'd stabs look'd like a breach in nature For ruin's wasteful[1] entrance: there, the murtherers, Steep'd[2] in the colours of their trade . . .

[1] *destructive*
[2] *soaked, dyed*

At this point Lady Macbeth cries out for help and faints. In all probability, she realises that her husband's hollow, melodramatic speech is likely to arouse suspicion rather than sympathy, and feigns her state of shock in order to distract attention. She is carried out, and Macbeth falls silent.

Banquo proposes that, when they are ready, they should all meet, calmly and formally, to investigate what has happened. There is fear and suspicion in the air, he says: he states, unequivocally, that he is against whoever has committed this evil and treacherous act. There is unanimous agreement.

All those present return to their chambers, with the exception of the dead King's heir, Malcolm, and his younger brother Donalbain. They know themselves to be innocent, but realise that the situation is extremely dangerous. They are likely to be prime suspects: worse still, the true murderer may well consider them his next target. They decide to escape at once, keeping apart for greater safety. Donalbain heads for Ireland, while Malcolm sets off for England.

Macbeth's ambition achieved

II, iv

Outside Macbeth's castle, later the same day, the Thane of Ross is talking to an old man about the terrible, unnatural events of the previous night.

Even now, in the daytime, the sky is dark and gloomy around the castle. It is as if nature itself has undergone a sudden, violent change. Strange, disturbing events were witnessed during the night of the murder:

Ross   ... Duncan's horses (a thing most strange and
                certain)
                Beauteous and swift, the minions[1] of their race,
                Turn'd wild in nature, broke their stalls, flung
                out,
                Contending 'gainst obedience, as[2] they would
                make
                War with mankind.

Old Man   'Tis said, they eat each other.
Ross   They did so; to th'amazement of mine eyes ...

[1] *favourites, finest examples*
[2] *as if*

Macduff joins them, bringing news of the morning's discussion at the castle. Although there was general agreement that Duncan was murdered by his servants, the flight of Malcolm and Donalbain has created the suspicion that the servants were acting under their orders.

With Duncan dead and his sons in hiding, it was necessary to nominate a new King of Scotland. Macbeth has been chosen, and is already on his way to the ancient capital, Scone, to be crowned. Macduff fears that things will change under the new King, and for the worse.

> *"The new king will be the man who has killed a king . . . The huge steam-roller of history has been put in motion and crushes everybody in turn. In* Macbeth, *however, this murder-cycle does not possess the logic of a mechanism, but reminds one rather of a frighteningly growing nightmare."*
>
> Jan Kott, *Shakespeare Our Contemporary*, 1965

One question remains unresolved

III, i

Macbeth and his wife are now King and Queen, residing in the royal palace at Forres. A state banquet is to take place in the evening, and many lords and noblemen, including Banquo, Ross and Lenox, are present at the palace.

At the moment, Banquo is alone, reflecting on Macbeth's progress:

Banquo   Thou hast it now, King, Cawdor, Glamis, all,
As the Weïrd Women promis'd; and, I fear,
Thou play'dst most foully for't . . .

So far, the witches' prophecies have come true; however, they also promised Banquo that his descendants, not Macbeth's, would be Kings. As Banquo is wondering whether to put any faith in the witches' words, Macbeth comes in, followed by the Queen and their courtiers.

Macbeth is friendly and expansive towards Banquo, reminding him of the evening's banquet. He establishes that Banquo is going out riding with his son Fleance this afternoon, and that they will be back an hour or two after dusk. He needs Banquo's advice, he says, but the matter can wait until tomorrow, when Banquo will have time. He mentions, pointedly, that Duncan's sons are spreading malicious rumours about him:

Macbeth   We hear, our bloody cousins[1] are bestow'd
In England, and in Ireland; not confessing
Their cruel parricide,[2] filling their hearers
With strange invention. But of that
   tomorrow . . .

[1] *Malcolm and Donalbain*
[2] *murder of their father*

Banquo leaves, and Macbeth graciously asks the others still present to give him some time on his own until they meet again for dinner.

Once he is alone, Macbeth's mood changes instantly. Although he is maintaining an affable manner in public, the insecurity of his position is tormenting him beyond endurance. This insecurity is caused by one man, whose awareness of the witches' prophecy makes him a constant threat:

Macbeth   To be thus is nothing, but to be safely thus:
Our fears in Banquo
Stick deep . . .

> *"Macbeth fears, envies, hates Banquo who has the reality of honour whereas he has but a mockery, a ghoulish dream of royalty. He envies Banquo's posterity their royal destiny won in terms of nature, not in terms of crime . . . Macbeth's agony is not properly understood till we realise his utter failure to receive any positive joy from the imperial magnificence to which he aspired."*
>
> G. Wilson Knight, *The Imperial Theme*, 1931

Banquo's behaviour has been dignified and irreproachable at all times; but this makes Macbeth fear him even more. The idea that it might be Banquo's descendants that rule Scotland is a source of constant anguish to him. It is he, Macbeth, who has taken the dreadful actions necessary to fulfil the prophecy, and it is fitting that his own descendants should succeed him:

Macbeth   Upon my head they plac'd a fruitless crown,
          And put a barren sceptre in my gripe . . .[1]
                  . . . If't be so,
          For Banquo's issue have I fil'd[2] my mind;
          For them the gracious Duncan have I
             murther'd . . .

[1] *grasp*
[2] *defiled, brutalised*

The prophecy may have come true so far, but Macbeth is determined that, on this point, the witches will be proved wrong. He knows that he will need to outwit fate itself: and he has already prepared a plan of action.

Another murder is planned

A servant comes in, bringing two unnamed visitors. Macbeth orders the servant to guard the door and make sure that no-one intrudes on their discussion.

Macbeth has already spoken in secrecy to the two men, both of whom have suffered personal catastrophe in recent times. He now emphasises the point that he has already tried to prove to them: that their misfortunes - which they had blamed on Macbeth - were caused, deliberately and systematically, by Banquo.

Macbeth now asks the men whether their patience and forgiveness are such that they can allow Banquo's persecution of them to go unpunished. He appeals to their manhood and courage: and he offers them the opportunity, through a single act, to get rid of their enemy, restore their own fortunes, and win the love and thanks of the King. He wants them to murder Banquo.

The two men have no qualms about carrying out the murder. They are both in such a desperate state that they have no interest in moral considerations, and Macbeth's elaborate justifications are wasted:

2nd Murderer   I am one, my Liege,
Whom the vile blows and buffets of the world
Hath so incens'd, that I am reckless[1] what
I do, to spite the world.

1st Murderer   And I another,
So weary with disasters, tugg'd[2] with fortune,
That I would set[3] my life on any chance,
To mend it, or be rid on't.

[1] *I don't care about the consequences*
[2] *worn out by wrestling*
[3] *risk*

> "He wants them to do the deed out of hatred for Banquo, and not out of the need of money, so that he himself shall be relieved of some part of the guilt . . ."
>
> Kenneth Muir, Introduction to the Arden Edition of *Macbeth*, 1984

Despite the murderers' readiness, Macbeth feels compelled to explain why Banquo's death is necessary, and how important it is that it should not be attributable to the King.

The murderers assure him that they will carry out his wishes, and Macbeth congratulates them on their courage. He tells them that the murder must be done tonight; he will give them details of the time and place shortly. It is imperative, he adds, that both Banquo and his son Fleance, who will be with him, are put to death. In the meantime, the murderers are to wait, unseen, within the royal palace.

Macbeth foresees a secure future

III, ii

Lady Macbeth, alone in her chamber, is reflecting unhappily on their present situation. Their ambition has been achieved, but they are living with a perpetual sense of insecurity and doubt. Her husband is constantly worried and withdrawn.

As Macbeth comes to join her, she questions him. They are not yet safe, he insists; the murder of Duncan was not enough.

Lady Macbeth How now, my Lord? why do you keep alone,
　　　　　　　Of sorriest fancies your companions making,
　　　　　　　Using[1] those thoughts, which should indeed
　　　　　　　　　have died
　　　　　　　With them they think on? Things without all
　　　　　　　　　remedy
　　　　　　　Should be without regard: what's done is done.
Macbeth　　We have scorch'd[2] the snake, not kill'd it:
　　　　　　　She'll close,[3] and be herself . . .

[1] *keeping company with*
[2] *slashed, wounded*
[3] *heal*

They cannot go on as they are, says Macbeth, living in fear and suffering from terrifying dreams every night; by contrast, the tranquillity of death seems preferable.

Macbeth reveals that he has planned a further dreadful action in order to give them complete security. He refuses to tell his wife what it is, but hints that it will take place, under cover of darkness, later today:

Lady Macbeth   What's to be done?

Macbeth   Be innocent of the knowledge, dearest chuck,
Till thou applaud the deed.
                     . . . Light thickens;[1] and the crow
Makes wing to th'rooky wood;
Good things of Day begin to droop and drowse,
Whiles Night's black agents to their preys do
    rouse.
Thou marvell'st at my words:[2] but hold thee
    still;
Things bad begun make strong themselves by
    ill.[3]

[1] *grows dim*
[2] *you are eager to know what I mean*
[3] *achievements gained through wrongdoing can only
be made secure by further acts of wickedness*

"One of the few strokes of pathos that are let soften the grimness of the tragedy is Lady Macbeth's wan effort to get near enough to the tortured man to comfort him. But the royal robes, stiff on their bodies - stiff as with caked blood - seem to keep them apart. He has grown a stranger to her . . ."

Harley Granville-Barker, Preface to *Macbeth*, 1923

The task remains unfinished

III, iii

The two murderers have received their instructions, and are lying in wait by the path leading to the palace. At the last minute, Macbeth has sent another man to join them. Like the other murderers, he remains anonymous: in all probability, he is a trusted henchman sent to spy on the activities of the two selected killers.

They hear horses approaching, and then a man's voice comes into earshot. They are sure it is Banquo, as all the other guests expected at the evening's banquet have already arrived. The horses seem to be moving away from them: the man who has just joined them explains that riders normally dismount at this point, and take a short cut to the palace on foot while their horses are taken along a separate path.

Banquo and Fleance now appear. The murderers hold up a light so that they can see their victims clearly. They recognise Banquo, and attack him savagely, stabbing him to death. Before dying, he just has time to cry out to Fleance, warning him to escape and, eventually, avenge his murder. Fleance runs off into the dark. One of the murderers has mistakenly put out the torch: the others call out for light so that they can find the boy and kill him. In the confusion, Fleance manages to escape.

Banquo's murder brings its consequences

III, iv

The royal banquet begins. To all appearances, the King and Queen are cordial, hospitable and good-humoured. Macbeth welcomes his guests and urges them to sit down; he himself intends to walk around the banquet table for a while, talking to his visitors individually.

A face appears at the door of the banquet hall. It is one of the murderers. Macbeth hurries over to speak to him. He learns with satisfaction that Banquo is dead, but the rest of the murderer's news fills him with bitter frustration:

Murderer	Most royal Sir . . . Fleance is scap'd.
Macbeth	Then comes my fit[1] again: I had else been perfect;
	Whole as the marble, founded as the rock,
	As broad and general as the casing air:[2]
	But now, I am cabin'd, cribb'd, confin'd . . .

[1] *gloom, depression*
[2] *as free and unconfined as the air around me*

Fleance will have to be dealt with in due course. Macbeth dismisses the murderer for the present: they will need to talk again soon.

Lady Macbeth calls her husband back to the banquet, and he quickly reassumes his polished, hospitable manner as he returns to join the company. He light-heartedly mentions Banquo's absence from the feast:

Macbeth	Here had we now our country's honour roof'd[1]
	Were the grac'd person of our Banquo present;
	Who may I rather challenge for unkindness,
	Than pity for mischance![2]

[1] *all the nobility of Scotland assembled under one roof*
[2] *who, I am sure, is late through thoughtlessness rather than misfortune*

Macbeth now makes his way to the table. He is taken aback; the table is full, and there is nowhere for him to sit. His reserved place is pointed out to him, and he is overcome with horror as he sees, sitting in his place, the ghost of Banquo, his face and body covered with deep gashes.

Macbeth's first reaction is to proclaim his innocence; it was not he who wielded the knife. His wife, thinking quickly, reassures their guests that he is suffering a temporary bout of confusion. He has long been prone to such attacks, she explains, and will recover in a few minutes. She appeals to everyone to ignore his strange behaviour:

Macbeth	Thou canst not say, I did it: never shake
	Thy gory locks at me.
Ross	Gentlemen, rise; his Highness is not well.
Lady Macbeth	Sit, worthy friends. My Lord is often thus,
	And hath been from his youth: pray you, keep seat;
	The fit is momentary; upon a thought
	He will again be well. If much you note him,[1]
	You shall offend him . . .

[1] *if you pay too much attention to his behaviour*

Lady Macbeth takes her husband aside angrily and tells him to pull himself together: he must put an end to these childish, fearful imaginings. Macbeth tries to convince his wife that the ghost is present, but it is invisible to all but himself.

He calms down a little as the ghost vanishes, but remains deeply shaken by the experience. There have always been murders in the past, and death has always been final: now, he muses, the dead are coming back to mingle with the living.

Lady Macbeth again calls her husband back to the banquet table. He apologises to his guests, explaining that his occasional fits of instability are insignificant and should be ignored. He asks for a drink, and proposes a toast to all those at the table, and to the absent Banquo, whose company they miss.

At this moment, Banquo's ghost reappears. Macbeth flies into an uncontrollable panic. He can face up to anything, he cries, except this terrifying, cold, deathly vision. As he pleads with the ghost to leave him alone, his wife tries desperately to maintain an atmosphere of normality, frantically urging the guests to disregard him.

Finally the ghost vanishes again, and Macbeth's terror subsides. He asks his wife in amazement how she manages to remain calm in the presence of such horrific sights. One of the guests, overhearing, enquires about the nature of the sights that the King has seen.

Lady Macbeth realises that the situation is out of hand. In his state of shock, her husband is likely to incriminate himself at any minute. She calls the banquet to an abrupt, unceremonious end:

Lady Macbeth I pray you, speak not; he grows worse and
worse;
Question enrages him. At once, good night: -
Stand not upon the order of your going,[1]
But go at once.

[1] *don't take the trouble to leave in your order of rank*

The banquet ends in disarray as the guests hurry out.

Macbeth sees the way forward

After the fateful banquet, Macbeth ponders on the consequences
of murder. It has always been believed, he reflects, that those
guilty of murder will, one way or another, be discovered and
punished:

Macbeth It will have blood, they say: blood will have
blood:
Stones have been known to move, and trees to
speak . . .

Lady Macbeth, weary and despondent after the traumatic
events of the evening, does not attempt to restrain her husband's
agitated thoughts.

Macbeth mentions that Macduff, the Thane of Fife, had de-
clined to come to the royal banquet. He is displeased. He knows
that Macduff had no valid reason to turn down his invitation;
in Macduff's household, as in those of all his Thanes and noblemen, he has paid a servant to supply him secretly with information.

Tomorrow, Macbeth will seek out the three witches again.

Whatever they say, he knows that more bloodshed may be necessary if he is to achieve personal security and suppress any signs of dissent. Indeed, he can see no other way out of his current predicament:

Macbeth   For mine own good,
            All causes[1] shall give way: I am in blood
            Stepp'd in so far, that, should I wade no more,
            Returning were as tedious as go o'er.

            [1] *all other considerations*

Lady Macbeth tells her husband that he is suffering from a lack of sleep, and the two of them retire for the night. Macbeth reassures her that things will get easier as time goes on: as yet, they are inexperienced in death.

"Macbeth dreams of the end of the nightmare, while sinking into it more and more. He dreams of a world without crime, while becoming enmeshed in crime more and more deeply. Macbeth's last hope is that the dead will not rise: but the dead do rise . . . Macbeth has dreamed of a final murder to end all murders. Now he knows: there is no such murder."

Jan Kott, *Shakespeare Our Contemporary*, 1965

Opposition starts to grow

III, v

Lenox is talking to another Scottish nobleman about Macbeth's murderous progress. The two men have established that they are in agreement, and are meeting in absolute secrecy: in the present atmosphere of fear and distrust, such talk is dangerous.

Lenox comments ironically on Macbeth's apparent affection for Duncan and Banquo, and on the flimsy evidence against the official suspects. He asks his companion about the whereabouts of Macduff, who is widely believed to be opposed to Macbeth's bloody rule.

The nobleman reveals that Macduff has secretly gone to England to meet King Edward, who is providing protection for Malcolm, Duncan's son and rightful successor. Macduff plans to ask the English King to help him raise an army, with the intention of removing Macbeth by force. Macbeth has heard rumours of military preparations in England, and is himself preparing for war. Suspicious of Macduff, he has already tried, without success, to summon him to the palace.

Lenox and his friend hope fervently that Macduff's mission is successful, and that an invading army will soon free Scotland from Macbeth's violent tyranny.

Witchcraft was taken extremely seriously in Shakespeare's time. King James I, the patron of Shakespeare's theatre company, took a strong personal interest in the subject, believing himself to have been the target of witchcraft on occasions. He attended a number of witchcraft trials and wrote extensively on the practices of witches, their detection and punishment. In the first year of his reign a law was passed specifically banning witchcraft:

". . . if any person shall use any invocation or conjuration of any evil or wicked spirit;

Or shall consult, covenant with, entertain, employ, feed or reward any evil or cursed spirit to or for any intent or purpose;

Or take up any dead man, woman or child out of the grave, or the skin, bone or any part of the dead person, to be employed or used in any manner of witchcraft, sorcery, charm or enchantment;

Or shall use, practise or exercise any sort of witchcraft, sorcery, charm or enchantment whereby any person shall be destroyed, killed, wasted, consumed, pined[1] or lamed in any part of the body;

That every such person being convicted shall suffer death."

[1] *weakened*

The mania for discovering and punishing witches was widespread and, at times, virtually uncontrolled. As an 18th-century commentator grimly observed:

". . . a sow could not be ill of the measles, nor a girl of the sullens, but some old woman was charged with witchcraft."

The law remained in force for over a hundred years, and countless thousands of suspected witches, and their defenders and sympathisers, were put to death.

Macbeth searches for answers

IV, i

The three witches meet again, in a hovel not far from Macbeth's royal palace. In their midst is a bubbling cauldron, and they chant spells as they toss a series of foul, potent and magical ingredients into the pot:

Witches	Double, double toil and trouble:
	Fire, burn; and, cauldron, bubble.
2nd Witch	Fillet of a fenny snake,[1]
	In the cauldron boil and bake;
	Eye of newt, and toe of frog,
	Wool of bat, and tongue of dog,
	Adder's fork, and blind-worm's sting,
	Lizard's leg, and howlet's[2] wing . . .

[1] *slice of a swamp-inhabiting snake*
[2] *young owl*

One of the witches senses that an evil presence is approaching, and it is at this point that Macbeth enters the hovel. He has some questions to which he is desperate to know the answers: he demands that the witches tell him the truth, at any cost.

The witches add further ingredients to the cauldron, and start to call up supernatural spirits to address Macbeth. There is a clap of thunder, and a man's head appears, its features hidden under a soldier's helmet. Macbeth tries to question the apparition, but the witches silence him. The disembodied head gives him a stark warning:

Macbeth   Tell me, thou unknown power, -
1st Witch   He knows thy thought:
             Hear his speech, but say thou nought.
1st Apparition Macbeth! Macbeth! Macbeth! beware Macduff;
             Beware the Thane of Fife . . .

Macbeth receives the warning gratefully. He tries to discover more from the apparition, but the witches tell him that the spirits cannot be questioned or commanded.

A second vision now appears, a new-born baby covered in blood, and addresses Macbeth. He takes hope from the message, but decides to take action of his own for complete security:

*2nd Apparition*Be bloody, bold and resolute: laugh to scorn
             The power of man, for none of woman born
             Shall harm Macbeth.
Macbeth   Then live, Macduff: what need I fear of thee?
             But yet I'll make assurance double sure,
             And take a bond of Fate:[1] thou shalt not
                 live . . .

   [1] *compel fate to keep its word*

Macbeth is encouraged again by the third apparition, a child wearing a crown and carrying a branch. It reassures him that he will rule in absolute safety until the trees themselves leave the ground and advance towards him:

3rd Apparition Be lion-mettled, proud, and take no care
             Who chafes, who frets, or where conspirers are:
             Macbeth shall never vanquish'd be, until
             Great Birnam wood to high Dunsinane hill
             Shall come against him.

However, one burning question remains. He asks the witches whether Banquo's descendants, and not his own, will rule over Scotland. The witches warn him that he has already asked enough, but he demands an answer.

A King now appears, resembling Banquo: another follows, and eventually a procession of eight Kings passes before Macbeth's eyes, filling him with impotent rage. Finally the ghost of Banquo himself, his face bloody from the knives of Macbeth's assassins, appears. He smiles as he indicates his royal descendants.

The witches mockingly bid farewell, and disappear. Exasperated and furious, Macbeth vows never again to become involved with them or believe their prophecies.

Lenox now arrives. He has followed Macbeth to pass on some news that has just arrived at the palace. Macduff is no longer to be found at his castle; he has fled to England. Macbeth is startled. Macduff, as the apparition said, is clearly dangerous. He realises that he should have disposed of him earlier, when he first had doubts about the Thane's loyalty. He resolves to act more swiftly in future:

Macbeth   From this moment,
                  The very firstlings[1] of my heart shall be
                  The firstlings of my hand.

    [1] *first-born: first impulses*

The first act he intends to carry out, with his new-found sense of purpose, is revenge upon Macduff.

Macbeth takes violent reprisals

IV, ii

Lady Macduff is distressed and angered by her husband's sudden, unannounced departure. She believes he has fled out of fear. Whatever the motive, she feels that his flight is foolish, as it will arouse suspicion even if he has done nothing to warrant it.

Ross has come to Macduff's castle in Fife, and is trying to comfort Lady Macduff. He knows more about her husband's disappearance than she does, but is unable to give away any details: like all the noblemen in Macbeth's court, he must be careful of what he says for fear of spies. Promising that he will be back soon, and reassuring her that Macduff is acting for the best, Ross takes his leave.

One of Lady Macduff's children is in the room with her, and she chatters with the boy, half in play, about his father's disappearance. The boy refuses to be downhearted: they will cope somehow, with or without a father.

A messenger rushes in. She and her children are in terrible danger, he warns. There is no time to say more, or to explain who he is: she must escape at once. As soon as he has given his warning, the man hurries away.

Lady Macduff is bewildered by the sudden warning. She knows she has done nothing wrong. This is no defence, she reflects sadly, in the real world. Before she has time to act, a gang of hired killers, sent by Macbeth, bursts into the room. They demand to know the whereabouts of the traitor Macduff.

The little boy cries out that his father is no traitor. The murderers attack him viciously: when he is dead, they pursue his mother out of the room. No-one in the castle is to be spared.

". . . the child, in its helplessness, defies the murderers. Its defiance testifies to the force which threatens Macbeth and which Macbeth cannot destroy."

Cleanth Brooks, *The Well Wrought Urn*, 1947

Macduff's loyalty is tested

IV, iii

Macduff has arrived at King Edward's palace, in England, hoping to gain support for military action against Macbeth. There he meets Malcolm, who has been staying with the King since the murder of his father Duncan.

The two men talk, sadly, of the state of Scotland. Macduff reports that the country is suffering dreadfully:

Macduff   Each new morn,
                New widows howl, new orphans cry . . .

Malcolm responds cautiously. He knows Macbeth to be a tyrant, but it would not be right for him to believe everything he hears. Besides, he cannot be sure of Macduff's motives; he may even have been sent by Macbeth as a spy.

Macduff says that his desperate desire to save Scotland has driven him to leave his wife and family: but even this, Malcolm points out, might be seen as suspicious.

In despair, Macduff decides to leave; Macbeth's position is secure if good men such as Malcolm will not offer any resistance. Malcolm reassures him that, despite his caution, he feels the same way as Macduff about the state of Scotland.

Malcolm's tone now changes suddenly. If he managed to defeat Macbeth and become King of Scotland, he reveals, his reign would be even more brutal:

Malcolm   . . . my poor country
          Shall have more vices than it had before,
          More suffer, and more sundry ways than ever,
          By him that shall succeed.
Macduff   What should he be?
Malcolm   It is myself I mean; in whom I know
          All the particulars of vice so grafted,
          That, when they shall be open'd,[1] black
              Macbeth
          Will seem as pure as snow . . .

          [1] when they come to flower

At first, Macduff is unmoved; it is inconceivable that the
gentle Malcolm could be comparable to the tyrannical, blood-
thirsty Macbeth. But Malcolm persists. He describes in detail
the lust, greed and violence that he looks forward, as King, to
enjoying.

Macduff tries to minimise and excuse the young man's faults,
believing that his virtues will outweigh them. Finally, however,
he is convinced that Malcolm's rule would be as devastating for
Scotland as Macbeth's. In an emotional outburst he denounces
Malcolm as being unfit to live, let alone govern Scotland. Angry
and bewildered, he recalls the goodness and piety of Malcolm's
parents:

Macduff   Thy royal father
          Was a most sainted King: the Queen, that bore
              thee,
          Oft'ner upon her knees than on her feet,
          Died every day she liv'd.[1]

          [1] lived every day of her life in preparation for God's
               judgement

Malcolm now reveals that he has been testing his friend's loyalty: none of his claims about his bad character are true. Macduff's passionate reaction has convinced Malcolm that he is trustworthy. He is sorry that the deceit should have been necessary; but on numerous occasions Macbeth has sent spies and agents to try to trick him and lure him into captivity.

Military preparations are already under way, Malcolm tells Macduff, and he asks his friend to join him in the battle against Macbeth. An army of ten thousand men, headed by Siward, Earl of Northumberland, is at their disposal. Macduff, who has barely recovered from his earlier fit of anger, is rendered almost speechless by this sudden, hopeful turn of events.

"This tragedy is one of the greatest creations of man . . . If we cannot make something great out of it, at least let us try to do something out of the ordinary."

Composer Giuseppe Verdi, writing to his librettist Francesco Piave in 1846, proposing the creation of an opera based on *Macbeth*.

Grim news from Scotland

A doctor enters the room and reports that King Edward will shortly be ministering, as he often does, to a group of wretched, sick people who have gathered outside the palace. The King has a mysterious ability to cure an illness - known as the Evil - which experienced doctors are unable to treat.

Malcolm tells Macduff that he has observed the process himself since arriving at King Edward's court, and that supernatural forces of goodness and healing seem to be involved:

Malcolm   How he solicits Heaven,
          Himself best knows; but strangely-visited[1]
               people,
          All swoln and ulcerous, pitiful to the eye,
          The mere despair of surgery,[2] he cures;
          Hanging a golden stamp[3] about their necks,
          Put on with holy prayers . . .

[1]   *afflicted*
[2]   *completely incurable by medical means*
[3]   *coin*

The 'King's Evil' was the name given to scrofula, a dis-
figuring disease of the lymph glands in the neck. The
belief that the monarch's touch could cure it lasted from
the reign of Edward the Confessor until well into the
18th century.

Many scholars believe that the brief episode mention-
ing King Edward's ability to heal the Evil was inserted
specially, as an indirect compliment, for a performance
of *Macbeth* given before King James I in 1606.

The Thane of Ross now arrives with news from Scotland.
The situation is worse than ever, he reports:

Macduff	Stands Scotland where it did?
Ross	Alas, poor country!

Almost afraid to know itself. It cannot
Be call'd our mother, but our grave; where
    nothing,
But who knows nothing,[1] is once seen to smile;
Where sighs, and groans, and shrieks that rent
    the air
Are made, not mark'd . . .[2]

[1] *no-one, except for those living in total ignorance*
[2] *noticed, remarked upon*

Macduff asks about his family, concerned that Macbeth's messengers, looking for him, may have distressed his wife and children. Ross is hesitant, and quickly changes the subject. The time for organised resistance has come, he says: on his return to Scotland, Macduff will provide inspiration and encouragement to others who wish to oppose Macbeth.

Malcolm mentions that an army of ten thousand men will soon be in Scotland to help the rebels. Ross is grateful, and wishes that his own tidings were equally good. He finds it almost impossible to break the news, but, pressed by his companions, finally blurts out his message: Macduff's entire family has been savagely wiped out.

Macduff is stunned into silence. Malcolm urges him to speak, and to transform his grief into determination to seek justice and revenge:

Malcolm	Give sorrow words; the grief, that does not speak,
	Whispers the o'er-fraught[1] heart, and bids it break.
Macduff	My children too?
Ross	Wife, children, servants, all That could be found.
Macduff	And I must be from thence![2] My wife kill'd too?
Ross	I have said.
Malcolm	Be comforted: Let's make us med'cines of our great revenge, To cure this deadly grief.
Macduff	He has no children. - All my pretty ones? Did you say all? - O Hell-kite![3]

[1] *overburdened*
[2] *absent, away from home*
[3] *hellish bird of prey*

Macduff is overwhelmed with anguish and sorrow, and racked with guilt that he was not present to protect his family. From this moment on, he has only one aim in life: to meet Macbeth, face to face, armed, in single combat.

The three men set off to take their leave of the King. Once that is done, they will return to Scotland, at the head of a great invading army, to confront Macbeth.

"All this passage is remarkably modern-sounding to twentieth-century ears . . . all twentieth-century tyrants have found it convenient, when an opponent of the regime has managed to get away to safety, to punish him by murdering the relatives who remain behind."

John Wain, *The Living World of Shakespeare*, 1964

Lady Macbeth is tormented by her memories

V, i

Macbeth and his wife are no longer at the royal palace, but at Dunsinane castle, Macbeth's military stronghold. Macbeth himself is with his army, trying to suppress the rebellions against his rule that have sprung up around the country.

Lady Macbeth's maidservant has become concerned about her mistress's behaviour. Many times, while still asleep, Lady Macbeth has gotten out of bed, walked about restlessly, carried out strange actions and spoken disturbing words. The maidservant has decided to summon a doctor to observe her.

It is night-time now, and the doctor is present. He questions the gentlewoman; she describes her mistress's actions when sleepwalking, but refuses to reveal what she has heard her say. The doctor reassures her that she can speak in confidence, but the gentlewoman remains adamant.

At this point Lady Macbeth emerges from her chamber. Her eyes are open, but she is fast asleep. She is carrying a candle. As her maidservant explains, she has developed an intense fear of the dark:

Gentlewoman . . . she has light by her continually; 'tis her
                command.

The two of them watch as Lady Macbeth starts to rub her hands together compulsively, as if she were washing them. She regularly does this, the gentlewoman explains, sometimes for as long as a quarter of an hour without stopping.

Lady Macbeth now starts to speak, and from the confused fragments of her speech the horror of what she has seen and done gradually emerges:

Lady Macbeth Out, damned spot! out, I say! - One; two: why, then 'tis time to do't. - Hell is murky. - Fie, my Lord, fie! a soldier, and afeard? - What need we fear who knows it, when none can call our power to accompt?[1] - Yet who would have thought the old man to have had so much blood in him?

[1] *accompt*

The doctor realises that they are witnessing the outpourings of a guilty conscience. Clearly she has been involved in some dreadful, murderous acts, and is beyond the help of medicine. She continues to rub her hands together desperately, crying out in anguish:

Lady Macbeth Here's the smell of blood still: all the perfumes of Arabia will not sweeten this little hand.

The doctor listens, aghast, as Lady Macbeth mentions the murder of Banquo. Finally she returns to bed, echoing the words she once used in an attempt to put her husband's mind at rest:

Lady Macbeth . . . come, give me your hand. What's done cannot be undone. To bed, to bed . . .

Here's the smell of blood still . . .

Blood is mentioned more than a hundred times in *Macbeth*, far more than in any other play by Shakespeare.

There is little the doctor can do: she needs spiritual rather than medical help, he observes grimly. He instructs the gentle-woman to keep a close eye on her and ensure that she is prevented from causing herself any injury. He leaves, knowing that he cannot reveal to anyone what he now suspects to be the truth.

Macbeth's opponents unite

V, ii

Most of Macbeth's Thanes and noblemen have by now deserted him. They have grouped together to form a rebel army and are now assembled near Dunsinane. News arrives that the English army, with Malcolm, Siward and Macduff at its head, is approaching. They will soon reach Birnam wood, about ten miles from Dunsinane castle. The rebels agree to join them immediately.

News also arrives of Macbeth. He has fortified Dunsinane castle in preparation for a siege, and is in a constant state of agitation and fury as his demoralised officers desert him and his power wanes:

Angus   Now does he feel
His secret murthers sticking on his hands;
Now minutely revolts upbraid his faith-breach:[1]
Those he commands move only in command,
Nothing in love: now does he feel his title
Hang loose about him, like a giant's robe
Upon a dwarfish thief.

> [1] *the constant rebellions against him are a harsh
> reminder of his own acts of treason*

The rebels set off for Birnam wood, determined to cleanse Scotland of the evil that has infected it since Macbeth's rise to power.

Macbeth is on edge

V, iii

In his castle at Dunsinane, Macbeth is pacing up and down rest-lessly, his mood changing by fits and starts. He has just received news that more of his Thanes have deserted him and joined forces with Malcolm.

He refuses to be shaken, reminding himself of what the spir-its, summoned by the three witches, have promised him. If they are right, he is surely invincible:

Macbeth   Bring me no more reports; let them fly all:[1]
             Till Birnam wood remove to Dunsinane,
             I cannot taint[2] with fear. What's the boy
                 Malcolm?
             Was he not born of woman?

            [1] *let all the Thanes desert me*
            [2] *weaken*

However, beneath his confidence there is an almost unbear-able tension, and when he sees fear in a servant's face he gives way to a moment of blind fury. Fear implies the possibility of defeat, and is utterly intolerable:

Macbeth   The devil damn thee black, thou cream-fac'd
                 loon![1]
             Where gott'st thou that goose look?

            [1] *rogue, fool*

The servant passes on the news that has made him pale: the invading army from England has been sighted, and it numbers ten thousand men. Macbeth orders the servant out of his sight, and his rage subsides. The coming battle will be decisive, he realises, and he is suddenly filled with deep, bitter regret, reflecting that he is condemned to unhappiness whatever the outcome:

Macbeth   I have liv'd long enough: my way of life
           Is fall'n into the sere, the yellow leaf;[1]
           And that which should accompany old age,
           As[2] honour, love, obedience, troops of friends,
           I must not look to have . . .

           [1] *has become withered and lifeless, like an autumn
               leaf*
           [2] *such as*

Calling for news of the invading army, he abandons his introspection and becomes ruthlessly purposeful. He orders his armour to be brought to him, even though the English have not yet approached: and he commands that soldiers are to be sent throughout the territory around the castle, executing anyone who expresses fear of the invaders.

Macbeth's attention now turns to the doctor, who is treating his wife. When told that there is no easy remedy for her agitation and sleeplessness, he quickly loses patience:

Macbeth	Canst thou not minister to a mind diseas'd,
	Pluck from the memory a rooted sorrow,
	Raze out the written troubles of the brain,
	And with some sweet oblivious antidote
	Cleanse the stuff'd[1] bosom of that perilous stuff
	Which weighs upon the heart?
Doctor	Therein the patient
	Must minister to himself.
Macbeth	Throw physic[2] to the dogs; I'll none of it.

[1] *burdened, troubled*
[2] *medicine*

He would truly respect the doctor's science, Macbeth remarks with grim humour, if his drugs and treatments could restore the health of Scotland and purge the country of the English invaders.

Macbeth is by now full of manic energy, and as he strides back and forth his servant tries unsuccessfully to help him on with his armour. As Macbeth rushes off, followed by his anxious servant, the doctor is left wishing that he had never come to Dunsinane.

Malcolm's forces head for Dunsinane

V, iv

The Scottish rebels and the English army have joined forces near Birnam wood. They are preparing to march towards Macbeth's castle on Dunsinane hill.

Malcolm is addressing the Thanes and generals at the head of the assembled troops. Unaware that Macbeth's spies have already established the size of the invading army, he gives an order that every soldier should cut down a branch from the nearby wood to use as camouflage:

Malcolm   Let every soldier hew him down a bough,
        And bear't before him: thereby shall we shadow[1]
        The numbers of our host, and make discovery[2]
        Err in report of us.

[1] *obscure, hide*
[2] *observation, reconnaissance*

The order is carried out, and the army proceeds towards Dunsinane. Spirits are high. The latest reports reveal that Macbeth's followers are utterly demoralised, and his army shrinking by the hour: deserters are making their escape whenever the opportunity arises.

> "... the steady forward march of ten thousand men, each carrying a green bough, is a wonderful visual symbol of the great tide of Nature flowing over the scene of Macbeth's crime, bringing healing and renewal."
>
> John Wain, *The Living World of Shakespeare*, 1964

Macbeth's hopes are shattered

V, v

Macbeth is preparing for a siege. He is confident that Dunsinane castle is secure and impregnable, but is frustrated that, with his depleted army, he cannot meet the enemy face to face:

Macbeth   Our castle's strength
            Will laugh a siege to scorn: here let them lie,
            Till famine and the ague[1] eat them up.
            Were they not forc'd[2] with those that should be
                ours,
            We might have met them dareful, beard to
                beard,
            And beat them backward home.

    [1] *fever*
    [2] *reinforced*

Suddenly, screaming is heard from another room in the castle. Macbeth, unmoved, sends an attendant to discover the cause. He remembers that such a sound would once have sent a wave of fear through him, and he realises that he has become immune to terror:

Macbeth   I have supp'd full with horrors:
            Direness, familiar to my slaughterous thoughts,
            Cannot once start me.[1]

    [1] *can no longer frighten me*

His attendant returns; Lady Macbeth is dead. In the desperation and confusion of the present, Macbeth is unable to feel grief. He remarks wistfully that her death should have happened at a different time and place, where such emotions could be felt freely. He sinks into profound despair as it dawns on him that all his attempts at working towards an imaginary future, like the attempts of people throughout history, have proved futile:

Macbeth	To-morrow, and to-morrow, and to-morrow,
	Creeps in this petty pace from day to day,[1]
	To the last syllable of recorded time;
	And all our yesterdays have lighted fools
	The way to dusty death.[2] Out, out, brief candle!
	Life's but a walking shadow; a poor player,
	That struts and frets his hour upon the stage,
	And then is heard no more: it is a tale
	Told by an idiot, full of sound and fury,
	Signifying nothing.

[1] *our continual preoccupation with the future makes our daily existence sluggish and meaningless*
[2] *hopes for the future, now consigned to history, have always provided a false sense of purpose to foolish humanity on its way to the grave*

". . . poet of the haunted imagination, Macbeth has to use the full tragic stride on his path between the three castles of Inverness, Forres and Dunsinane. For much of the way he is on a narrow bridge across the depths of hell. The verse falls in flakes of fire . . ."

J. C. Trewin, *Going to Shakespeare*, 1978

A messenger enters. He is hesitant: Macbeth, irritable and impatient, tells him to deliver his news. The man tells him that, while observing the English army near Birnam, he has seen a bizarre sight. Malcolm's army, camouflaged with branches, is advancing:

Messenger   . . . I look'd toward Birnam, and anon,[1]
                 methought,
              The wood began to move.

[1] *suddenly*

Macbeth is devastated. The apparition summoned by the witches had promised him that he was invincible; nothing could harm him until Birnam wood itself marched up the hill towards Dunsinane. The impossible is now happening, and he flies into a frenzy of anger and panic. He decides, impulsively, that his only safety lies in action, and he orders all his troops out of the castle.

They are to confront the approaching army out in the field, rather than remain trapped in Dunsinane castle. If they are to die, they will die fighting.

Macbeth survives the first attempt

V, vi - vii

Malcolm's army is now in view of Dunsinane castle. He orders his troops to drop the branches they have been carrying.

The English general Siward and his son lead the first wave of troops, as planned, with Malcolm and Macduff heading the next battalion. As they approach, Macbeth's troops flood out of the castle, and the two sides join battle.

On the battlefield, Macbeth realises that there is no escape: he must face the enemy and fight his way to safety. Despite everything, there is one prophecy still protecting him. He repeats to himself the words of the bloody new-born baby summoned by the witches:

Macbeth They have tied me to a stake: I cannot fly,
      But, bear-like, I must fight the course.[1] -
       What's he,
      That was not born of woman? Such a one
      Am I to fear, or none.

     [1] *face the onslaught, like a chained bear facing a*
      pack of dogs

> *. . . bear-like, I must fight the course.*
>
> A few minutes' walk from the Globe Theatre, where many of Shakespeare's plays were first performed, was the Bear Garden, a large open-air arena. A German traveller of the time describes a visit:
>
> *"Without the city are some theatres, where English actors represent almost every day comedies and tragedies to very numerous audiences . . . There is still another place, built in the form of a theatre, which serves for the baiting of bears and bulls. They are fastened behind, and then worried by those great English dogs and mastiffs . . . To this entertainment there often follows that of whipping a blinded bear, which is performed by five or six men, standing in a circle with whips, which they exercise upon him without any mercy. He cannot escape from them because of his chains . . ."*
>
> Paul Hentzner, *Travels in England*, 1598

Siward's youthful son now comes upon Macbeth, and challenges him fearlessly. The two of them fight, and the young man is slain. Macbeth is heartened; the prophecy is holding good. He quickly starts to regain confidence in his invincibility.

Macduff, hearing the men's shouts, comes in search of Macbeth, but he has moved on. Macduff has no quarrel with Macbeth's followers or mercenaries: his only desire is to track down the tyrant himself and avenge the murder of his wife and children. Fervently hoping that the opportunity will not be denied him, he continues his search of the battlefield.

Outside the castle itself, Siward reports to Malcolm that Macbeth's forces are on the verge of defeat. The castle has been surrendered with little resistance, and he invites Malcolm to enter.

Macduff's wish is fulfilled

V, viii

By now Macbeth realises that defeat is inevitable. Nevertheless, he is determined to cause as much bloodshed as possible amongst the enemy troops, and he sets off into the thick of the battle.

Suddenly he hears a voice behind him. It is the one man whom the spirits warned him to beware. Macduff has finally caught up with his quarry:

Macduff	Turn, Hell-hound, turn!
Macbeth	Of all men else I have avoided thee:
	But get thee back, my soul is too much charg'd
	With blood of thine already.
Macduff	I have no words;
	My voice is in my sword . . .

The two men struggle violently. Macduff fails to wound his opponent, and Macbeth taunts him, revealing the supernatural reassurance that he has been given. Macduff's answer unnerves him utterly:

Macbeth	Thou losest labour . . .[1]
	I bear a charmed life; which must not yield
	To one of woman born.
Macduff	Despair thy charm;
	And let the Angel, whom thou still hast serv'd,[2]
	Tell thee, Macduff was from his mother's womb
	Untimely ripp'd.

[1] *you are wasting effort*
[2] *the demon that you have always followed*

Macduff was not born of a living woman: his mother had died in pregnancy, and her lifeless body was cut open to free the baby within.

Macbeth's last hope is dashed. He curses the witches and spirits for their ambiguous, deceptive promises. His courage deserts him, and he refuses to fight. It is now Macduff's turn to taunt his opponent. If Macbeth surrenders, he says, he will live in permanent captivity, no longer a King but an object of ridicule and hatred.

Macbeth, spurred into action, decides to fight. The first of the witches' apparitions, a disembodied head, had warned him to beware Macduff: he now has no choice but to put it to the test. He crosses swords with Macduff, and prepares to fight to the death:

Macbeth   . . . lay on, Macduff;
> And damn'd be him that first cries, 'Hold, enough!'

> "*. . . it is at his own risk that Macbeth, who has been so apt to create a false impression, should take the witches' other statements at face value. It is Macbeth's powers of self-deception that bring about his final overthrow.*"
>
> Stanley Wells, *Shakespeare: A Dramatic Life*, 1994

The battle is over

V, ix

In Dunsinane castle, Malcolm, Siward and the rebel leaders are assembled, anxiously awaiting news of the day's casualties. Macduff is missing, as is Siward's son.

News now arrives of young Siward, whose fearless but unsuccessful encounter with Macbeth has been witnessed:

Ross   Your son, my Lord, has paid a soldier's debt:
He only liv'd but till he was a man;
The which no sooner had his prowess confirm'd,
In the unshrinking station where he fought,[1]
But like a man he died.

> [1] *by the fact that he remained firmly where he stood, without retreating*

Ross and Malcolm are greatly upset by the young man's death, but Siward responds stoically; he is an old soldier himself, and his son has died an honourable death, one that might be expected of any soldier in battle.

Macduff now returns. He carries Macbeth's severed head on a pole. He addresses Malcolm, the rightful heir to the throne:

Macduff   . . . the time is free.
I see thee compass'd with thy kingdom's pearl,[1]
That speak my salutation in their minds;
Whose voices I desire aloud with mine, -
Hail, King of Scotland!

> [1] *surrounded by the noblemen of Scotland, who are like the pearls encircling a crown*

Malcolm is unanimously acclaimed King of Scotland. Macbeth and his Queen - who, it now emerges, took her own life - are dead. There is much to do, says Malcolm. Those who have helped him will be rewarded; those who have fled from persecution must be welcomed back to Scotland; and those who helped to implement Macbeth's evil rule must be brought to justice.

Everything will be done in good time. A new age is dawning, and the nation, freed from oppression, will finally be restored to health and prosperity.

> "Blood will cease to flow, movement will recommence, fear will be forgotten, sleep will season every life, and the seeds of time will blossom in due order. The circle of safety which Shakespeare has drawn around his central horror is thinly drawn, but it is finely drawn and it holds."
>
> Mark Van Doren, *Shakespeare*, 1939

ACKNOWLEDGEMENTS

The following publications have proved invaluable as sources of factual information and critical insight:

W. H. Auden, *The Dyer's Hand*, Faber and Faber, 1963

Charles Boyce, *Shakespeare A to Z*, Roundtable Press, 1990

A. C. Bradley, *Shakespearean Tragedy*, Macmillan, 1904

Cleanth Brooks, *The Well Wrought Urn*, Harcourt, Brace & Co., 1947

Levi Fox, *The Shakespeare Handbook*, Bodley Head, 1987

Harold C. Goddard, *The Meaning of Shakespeare*, University of Chicago Press, 1951

Harley Granville-Barker, Preface to the Players' Shakespeare edition of *Macbeth*, Ernest Benn, 1923

Germaine Greer, *Shakespeare*, from the *Past Masters* series, edited by Keith Thomas, Oxford University Press, 1986

Alan Hobson, *Full Circle: Shakespeare and Moral Development*, Chatto & Windus, 1972

Ted Hughes, *Shakespeare and the Goddess of Complete Being*, Faber and Faber, 1992

G. Wilson Knight, *The Imperial Theme*, Oxford University Press, 1931

Jan Kott, *Shakespeare Our Contemporary*, Doubleday, 1965

Kenneth Muir, Introduction to the Arden edition of *Macbeth*, Methuen, 1984

Laurence Olivier, *On Acting*, Weidenfeld and Nicholson, 1986

Robert Speaight, *Shakespeare: The Man and his Achievement*, Dent, 1977

Peter Thomson, *Shakespeare's Professional Career*, Cambridge University Press, 1992

J. C. Trewin, *Going to Shakespeare*, Allen & Unwin, 1978

Mark Van Doren, *Shakespeare*, Henry Holt, 1939

John Wain, *The Living World of Shakespeare: A Playgoer's Guide*, Macmillan, 1964

Stanley Wells, *Shakespeare: A Dramatic Life*, Sinclair-Stevenson, 1994

John Dover Wilson, *Life in Shakespeare's England*, Cambridge University Press, 1911

All quotations from *Macbeth* are taken from the Arden Shakespeare.